FISH AND SEAFOOD COOKING

Edited by Jane Solmson

Library of Congress Catalog card number: 78-66262
ISBN: 0-517-276666
Published under arrangement with Ottenheimer Publishers, Inc.
Printed in the United States of America.

Contents

Introduction

Fish and Seafood is for those picky eaters who say they don't like fish because it tastes too fishy. It is just the book for those seafood lovers who think you can only get good seafood dishes at expensive restaurants. Mostly, it is the perfect combination of over 100 recipes for anyone who likes delicious meals with all types of fish and shellfish.

By following the simple instructions, anyone can create dishes that will please the palate of the pickiest gourmet. Using tuna, halibut, scallops or lobster, even a beginner can prepare hors d'oeuvres, salads, casseroles and main dishes that will send a flood of compliments directly to the chef.

Cooks on a tight budget will love the economical and tasty recipes for soups and seafood pies. Calorie counters will be surprised at how few calories can be contained in dishes with so much flavor. Have lots of fun creating dishes of fish and seafood that will always be remembered with a smile.

HORS D'OEUVRES

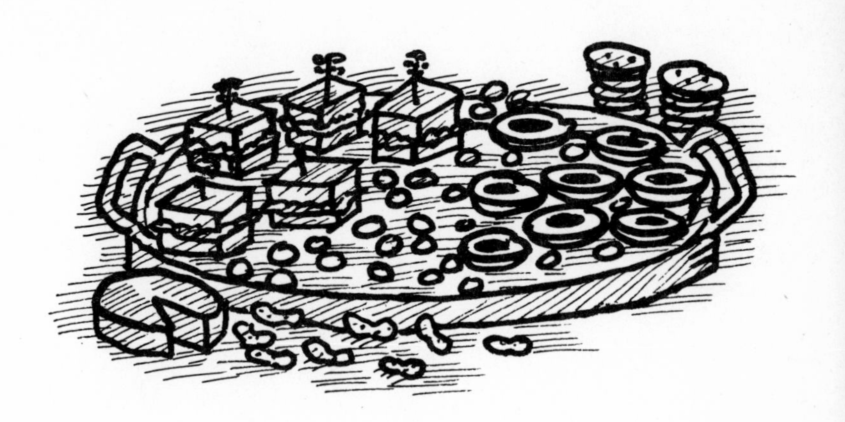

hot clam tarts

Pastry for 2-crust 9-inch pie
2 tablespoons butter or margarine
2 tablespoons flour
1 cup light cream
½ teaspoon salt
¼ teaspoon Tabasco pepper sauce
2 teaspoons dry sherry
¼ cup grated Parmesan cheese, divided
1 cup minced clams (2 8-ounce cans, drained)

Roll out pastry, cut into 2½-inch squares. Line small 1¼-inch muffin pans with squares of pastry; prick with tines of fork.

Bake in 425°F oven 10 minutes or until crisp and golden brown. Remove shells from pans; set aside.

In small saucepan melt butter; blend in flour. Stir in cream, salt, Tabasco, sherry and 3 tablespoons Parmesan cheese. Cook, stirring constantly, until thickened. Add clams; heat.

Spoon into tart shells; sprinkle with remaining Parmesan cheese. Return to 350°F oven 5 minutes to heat. Serve immediately. About 3 dozen miniature tarts.

shrimp wrapped in bacon

8 cleaned shrimp with tails intact
8 slices bacon

Wrap shrimp with bacon; fasten with toothpicks. Bake in 350°F oven 15 to 20 minutes. Serve as an appetizer. Serves 4.

stuffed clams

2 dozen clams (littleneck or rock)
3/4 cup dry white wine
1/4 cup water
1/2 teaspoon salt
3 tablespoons olive oil
1/2 cup chopped onion
1/2 cup raw long-grain rice
1/4 teaspoon pepper
1/2 teaspoon allspice
1/4 teaspoon cinnamon
3 tablespoons currants
3 tablespoons pine nuts
2 tablespoons chopped parsley

stuffed clams

Scrub clams; soak them in several changes of cold water to remove sand. Place in a skillet with wine, water, and salt. Cover and steam 10 minutes, until shells open. Discard any clams that do not open. Cool; remove clams from shells. Save shells; strain pan juices.

In a medium saucepan heat oil and sauté onion until golden. Add rice and 1 cup pan juices. Bring to a boil. Cover; reduce heat to low. Cook 15 minutes. Add pepper, spices, currants, pine nuts, and parsley. Cook 5 minutes. Cool. Dice clams; add to pilaf.

Stuff shells with rice mixture; chill. Serve as an appetizer. 24 appetizers.

angels on horseback

1 can (12 ounces) oysters, fresh or frozen
2 tablespoons chopped parsley
1/2 teaspoon salt
Paprika
Pepper
10 slices bacon, cut in thirds

Thaw frozen oysters. Drain oysters. Sprinkle with parsley and seasonings. Place an oyster on each piece of bacon. Wrap bacon around oyster; secure with a toothpick.

Place oysters on a broiler pan. Broil about 4 inches from source of heat 8 to 10 minutes or until bacon is crisp. Turn carefully. Broil 4 to 5 minutes longer or until bacon is crisp. Approximately 30 hors d'oeuvres.

caviar crown

1 jar (4 ounces) salmon caviar
1 jar (3½ ounces) whitefish caviar
2 packages (8 ounces each) cream cheese, softened
2 tablespoons lemon juice
2 tablespoons chopped green onion
1 teaspoon Worcestershire sauce
Parsley
Assorted party breads or melba toast

Drain caviars. Cream the cheese and seasonings. Place cheese mixture in center of a serving plate; shape in a circle about 7 inches in diameter and 1 inch thick, similar to a layer cake. Cover a 4-inch circle in the center with salmon caviar. Cover the remaining 1½ inches on top and sides with whitefish caviar.

Place small sprigs of parsley around edge of salmon caviar. (A ring of overlapping slices of tiny stuffed olives or a ribbon of cream cheese put through a pastry tube may be substituted for the parsley.)

Garnish base of cheese mixture with parsley. Serve with party breads or melba toast. Makes approximately 2 cups.

anchovy sticks

10 slices bread, toasted and buttered
½ cup chopped green onions
½ cup chopped parsley
40 anchovy fillets
¼ pound butter

Cut each piece of buttered toast into 4 1-inch strips.

Mix together chopped onions and parsley. Sprinkle mixture over toast strips. Top with 1 anchovy fillet on each toast stick; dot with butter.

Bake sticks at 375°F just long enough to heat through. (The best way to be sure this appetizer is just right is to try one—but you may want to eat the whole batch!)

Serve sticks hot; allow 2 or 3 sticks per person. Makes 40 sticks.

clam macadamia puffs

1 8-ounce package cream cheese, softened
1 can minced clams, drained
1 teaspoon green onion, minced
½ cup chopped macadamia nuts
Salt to taste
Dash of red pepper
¾ teaspoon Worcestershire sauce
1 tablespoon ground macadamia nuts
1 teaspoon paprika

Whip cheese thoroughly; add clams, mixing well. Add onion, chopped macadamias, salt, red pepper and Worcestershire sauce; whip again, testing for salt. Refrigerate in a covered dish.

When ready to serve, heap the mixture generously on salty crackers; bake 20 minutes in 300°F oven. Decorate with sprinkle of ground macadamias and paprika. Makes approximately 20.

oysters rockefeller

2 tablespoons chopped green onion
2 tablespoons chopped celery
3 tablespoons chopped fennel (optional)
3 tablespoons chopped parsley
¼ pound butter
1 cup watercress or spinach
3 tablespoons bread crumbs
3 tablespoons Pernod or anisette
¼ teaspoon salt
⅛ teaspoon white pepper
Dash cayenne
2 dozen oysters on the half shell

Sauté onion, celery, and herbs in 3 tablespoons butter for 3 minutes. Add watercress or spinach; let it wilt. Place this mixture, remaining butter, bread crumbs, liqueur, and seasonings into blender. Blend for 1 minute.

Put 1 tablespoon mixture on each oyster. Place oyster shells on rock-salt beds; dampen the salt slightly.

Bake at 450°F about 4 minutes or until butter is melted and oysters are heated. Serves 4.

clams casino

2 dozen cherrystone clams
2 tablespoons olive oil
1 tablespoon butter
½ cup finely minced onion
¼ cup finely chopped green pepper
2 cloves garlic, peeled and chopped
1 cup dry bread crumbs
4 slices crisp bacon, crumbled
½ teaspoon dried oregano, crumbled
2 tablespoons grated Parmesan cheese
Parsley flakes and paprika
Olive oil

Wash and scrub clams well to remove grit. Place on a baking sheet; place in a 450°F oven until shells open. Remove meat from shell and chop. Reserve the chopped clams; discard ½ of the shells.

Heat oil and butter in a small skillet. Add onion, pepper and garlic; sauté until tender. Remove from heat; cool. Add bread crumbs, bacon, oregano, Parmesan cheese, and reserved clams; mix well.

Fill clam shells with mixture. Sprinkle with parsley flakes and paprika; drizzle with olive oil. Bake in a 450°F oven until lightly browned (about 7 minutes). Serves 6, hot.

lobster boats

½ pound cooked lobster meat, fresh or frozen
24 fresh mushrooms, approximately 1½ inches in diameter
¼ cup condensed cream of mushroom soup
2 tablespoons fine soft bread crumbs
2 tablespoons mayonnaise or salad dressing
¼ teaspoon Worcestershire sauce
⅛ teaspoon liquid hot pepper sauce
Dash of pepper
Grated Parmesan cheese

Thaw frozen lobster meat. Drain lobster meat. Remove any remaining shell or cartilage. Chop lobster meat. Rinse mushrooms in cold water. Dry mushrooms; remove stems.

Combine soup, crumbs, mayonnaise, seasonings, and lobster. Stuff each mushroom cap with a tablespoonful of the lobster mixture. Sprinkle with cheese.

Place mushrooms on a well-greased baking pan, 15 × 10 × 1 inch. Bake in a hot oven, 400°F, 10 to 15 minutes or until lightly browned. 24 hors d'oeuvres.

stuffed mushrooms

8 ounces cooked crab, shrimp, or lobster, minced
4 water chestnuts, minced
1 scallion, minced
2 teaspoons soy sauce
1 teaspoon dry sherry
1 teaspoon sugar
1 teaspoon cornstarch
1 egg
12 mushroom stems, minced and browned in a little oil
12 large mushrooms, stems removed
Parsley (optional)

Combine minced crab, chestnuts, and scallion with remaining ingredients. Fill mushroom caps with the mixture; bake at 350°F 20 minutes. Serve hot garnished with parsley. 12 appetizers.

skewered shrimp

1 pound frozen raw, peeled, cleaned shrimp
2 large green peppers
8 slices bacon, cut in sixths
3 cans (4 ounces each) button mushrooms, drained
⅓ cup melted fat or oil
1 teaspoon salt
Dash of pepper

Thaw frozen shrimp. Rinse with cold water. Wash green peppers; cut into 1-inch squares.

Alternate shrimp, bacon, mushrooms, and green pepper on 48 skewers or round toothpicks, approximately 3 inches long. Place kabobs on a well-greased broiler pan.

Combine remaining ingredients. Brush kabobs with sauce. Broil about 4 inches from source of heat 5 to 7 minutes. Turn carefully; brush with sauce. Broil 5 to 7 minutes longer, basting once. Approximately 48 hors d'oeuvres.

scal-la-pops

1 pound scallops, fresh or frozen
1 can (5 ounces) water chestnuts, drained
Marinade
15 slices bacon, cut in half

Thaw frozen scallops. Rinse with cold water to remove any shell particles. Cut large scallops in half. Cut water chestnuts in thirds. Place scallops and water chestnuts in a bowl.

Pour marinade over; let stand at least 2 hours. Stir occasionally. Drain. Place a scallop and a piece of water chestnut on each piece of bacon. Wrap bacon around scallop; secure with a toothpick.

Place scallops on a broiler pan. Broil about 4 inches from source of heat 8 to 10 minutes or until bacon is crisp. Turn carefully. Broil 4 to 5 minutes longer or until bacon is crisp. Approximately 30 hors d'oeuvres.

marinade
¼ cup salad oil
¼ cup soy sauce
2 tablespoons catsup
1 tablespoon vinegar
¼ teaspoon pepper
2 cloves garlic, crushed

Combine all ingredients; mix thoroughly. Approximately ¾ cup of marinade.

party salmon ball

1-pound can salmon
8 ounces cream cheese, room temperature
1 tablespoon lemon juice
2 teaspoons grated onion
1 teaspoon prepared horseradish
¼ teaspoon salt
3 drops liquid smoke
½ cup chopped pecans

Drain salmon; flake carefully with fork or your fingers.

Combine salmon with softened cream cheese; add lemon juice, onion, horseradish, salt, and liquid smoke. Mix thoroughly; cover bowl; refrigerate a few hours until firm.

Shape salmon into a ball; roll in chopped nuts. Wrap tightly in plastic wrap; return to refrigerator until serving. Serve with firm unflavored crackers.

fish balls for a party

fish balls for a party

2 pounds frozen haddock fillets
1 cup cracker meal
2 teaspoons salt
Dash of white pepper
1½ cups light cream
Fat for deep frying
Parsley and paprika for garnish
1 lemon, sliced

Put haddock, partially thawed, through a food grinder twice. Place it in a large bowl. Add cracker meal, salt, pepper, and cream. Mix until smooth.

Now, put your hands under cold water. With moist hands, shape fish mixture into 1-inch balls.

Heat fat in medium skillet; using a slotted spoon, drop fish balls into fat. Allow to simmer 10 minutes. Remove cooked fish balls with slotted spoon; drain on paper towels. Cook rest of balls in same way.

Put fish balls on a heated platter and sprinkle with parsley and paprika; garnish with lemon slices. Keep toothpicks handy for picking up these delicacies. 24 to 36 balls.

pickled mackerel

3 red onions
1 cup plus 1½ tablespoons vinegar
Dash of salt
20 peppercorns
2 bay leaves
4 whole mackerels
1 bunch dill, chopped

Peel onions; slice into rings.

In a pot boil the vinegar, salt, peppercorns, and bay leaves. Set aside to cool.

Wash, clean, fillet, and halve the mackerels. Cut each piece in half again. Dry them thoroughly.

Put fillets into a glass pot. Cover them with onion rings. Spread the marinade on top of that. Let stand for at least 24 hours.

Serve the mackerel with chopped dill. Makes 16 pieces.

pickled mackerel

SOUPS AND STEWS

shrimp bisque

2 pounds shrimp
3 cups chicken stock
3 tablespoons butter
1 onion, sliced
1 carrot, sliced
1 stalk celery, sliced
3 tablespoons rice
1 bay leaf
3 to 4 sprigs of parsley (or 1 tablespoon dried parsley)
Squeeze of lemon juice
1/4 teaspoon ground mace
1 cup heavy cream
3 tablespoons brandy or sherry

Remove shells from shrimp; wash in cold water. Reserve ½ cup shrimp for garnish. Put shells into a pan with stock; simmer gently 20 minutes.

Melt butter; cook onion, carrot and celery 4 to 5 minutes to soften. Add rice, shrimp (roughly chopped), herbs, lemon juice and seasoning. Cook together 1 minute. Strain over the stock. Bring to a boil; simmer 20 minutes.

Remove bay leaf. Put soup into electric blender; blend until smooth; or put through a fine food mill or sieve.

Return soup to pan; add reserved ½ cup shrimp. Reheat and adjust seasoning. Add heated cream, and, just before serving, add the brandy or sherry. Serves 4 to 6, hot.

mediterranean fish stew

broth

1 large fish head
1 bay leaf
1 medium onion, chopped
½ teaspoon salt
¼ teaspoon white pepper
6 cups water

stew

1 large onion, chopped
1 clove garlic, minced
1 tablespoon white wine
1 tablespoon water
3 medium potatoes, peeled and cubed
1 pound whitefish fillets, cut into cubes
2 tablespoons lemon juice
3 medium tomatoes, peeled and chopped
¼ cup stuffed green olives
1 tablespoon capers
Salt and white pepper to taste
Chopped parsley for garnish

In a 4-quart saucepan, combine ingredients for broth; simmer 1 hour. Strain; reserve broth.

Cook onion and garlic in wine and water until soft. Add fish broth and potatoes; simmer 30 minutes.

Sprinkle fish with lemon juice; add to broth 10 minutes before end of cooking time. After 5 minutes add tomatoes, olives, and capers. Season to taste; sprinkle with parsley. Serves 4.

seafood stew

sauce

2 tablespoons vegetable oil
2 onions, chopped, or 3 leeks, sliced
4 cloves garlic, crushed
2 fresh tomatoes, peeled and diced
3 tablespoons tomato paste
2 cups bottled clam juice
4 cups chicken bouillon
1 tablespoon salt
⅛ teaspoon pepper
¼ teaspoon saffron
½ teaspoon thyme
1 bay leaf
6 sprigs parsley
Grated rind of 1 orange

seafoods

1 2-pound lobster and/or other shellfish
2 pounds assorted whitefish fillets
Chopped parsley

Heat vegetable oil in large saucepan or Dutch oven. Sauté onions or leeks several minutes, until translucent. Add remaining sauce ingredients; simmer 45 minutes.

Prepare seafoods by cooking lobster. (Place in kettle of boiling salted water 10 minutes.) Break claws and tail from body; crack claws; cut tail into 1-inch chunks. Remove black vein from tail pieces; leave shell on meat. Wash; cut fish fillets into 2-inch pieces. Add lobster and firm-fleshed fish (sea bass, perch, etc.) to boiling sauce. Boil rapidly 5 minutes; add tender-fleshed fish, such as clams, scallops, sole, or cod. Boil another 5 minutes. Lift seafoods out as soon as cooked; keep them warm in soup tureen or platter. Boil liquid 10 minutes to reduce. Strain liquid through coarse sieve into tureen, mashing through some of the vegetables. Garnish with parsley. Serves 6.

mediterranean fish stew

manhattan clam chowder

4 ounces salt pork or bacon, cut into small pieces
1 cup minced onion
2 tablespoons finely chopped flat-leaf parsley
½ teaspoon freshly ground black pepper
½ bay leaf
2 cups minced celery
1 cup minced green pepper
3 cans (16 ounces each) minced clams
2 bottles (8 ounces each) clam juice
1 can (1 pound, 12 ounce) Italian-style tomatoes, drained and chopped (save liquid)
4 cups finely diced potatoes
8 cups water
Salt and pepper to taste
2 tablespoons butter
Chopped parsley for garnish

In a heavy soup pot, cook salt pork or bacon with onion, parsley, and black pepper until pork starts to render fat. Stir; cook 5 minutes. Add bay leaf, celery, and green pepper; cook 15 minutes.

Add juice from minced clams, one bottle clam juice, liquid from tomatoes, potatoes, water, and seasonings. Simmer 25 minutes.

Add clams, chopped tomatoes, and second bottle of clam juice. Correct seasonings; add butter, sprinkle top with parsley, and serve with crusty bread or garlic bread, or with oyster crackers sprinkled with melted butter and heated 2 to 3 minutes under broiler. Serves 8.

maryland crab soup

6 cups strong beef stock
3 cups mixed vegetables (fresh, leftover or frozen—include chopped onions and celery, diced carrots, peas, lima beans, cut string beans, corn, okra and tomatoes; not squash, cabbage or potatoes)
1 pound crab meat (claw or white meat)
Seafood seasoning to taste
Claws and pieces of whole crab if available (either raw or cooked)

Heat stock in a large soup pot. Add vegetables and seasoning, simmer 1 hour.

Add crab meat, crab claws, and pieces (if available) 30 minutes before serving. Simmer gently, to heat through and allow flavors to blend.

Serve hot in large soup bowls, with bread and butter or hard crusty rolls and butter as accompaniment. Serves 4 to 6, hot.

SALADS AND MOLDS

trout in lemon aspic

4 whole fresh lake trout (scaled, viscerated, and cleaned)
1½ cups white wine
1 cup chicken consommé
3 tablespoons lemon juice
2 tablespoons dry sherry
1 small onion, cut into rings
3 sprigs parsley
1½ envelopes unflavored gelatin (1½ tablespoons)
¼ cup water
¼ cup chopped parsley
1 lemon, thinly sliced and seeds removed

Place trout in a 12-inch baking dish. Add white wine, consommé, lemon juice, sherry, onion, and parsley sprigs. Cover with lid or foil; gently simmer until fish flakes (about 20 minutes).

While fish is cooking, soak gelatin in cold water.

Lift trout from baking dish; carefully remove skin. Discard parsley sprigs from stock; add gelatin mixture and chopped parsley. Heat again until hot but not boiling.

Pour aspic into a serving dish; cool slightly. Arrange fish in serving dish before aspic has set. Place 2 onion rings on top of each trout. Arrange lemon slices in dish; spoon aspic over all. Chill 4 hours before serving. Serves 4.

molded tuna salad

1 envelope unflavored gelatin
¼ cup cold water
¾ cup hot water
2 tablespoons lemon juice
1 teaspoon prepared mustard
¼ teaspoon paprika pepper
Salt to taste
2 cans (6½ to 7 ounces each) tuna fish
1 cup chopped celery
½ cup whipped cream
Lettuce

dressing
½ cup mayonnaise
¼ cup finely diced cucumber
1 tablespoon chopped green pepper
1 teaspoon tarragon vinegar
Dash of cayenne pepper

Soften gelatin in cold water 5 to 10 minutes; add hot water; stir until gelatin has melted. Add lemon juice, mustard, paprika and salt to taste. Set aside to chill until partially set.

Add drained and flaked tuna and celery; fold in whipped cream. Spoon into individual molds; chill until set. Turn out on a bed of lettuce.

Combine all ingredients for Dressing; serve separately. Serves 5 to 6.

niçoise salad

8 small potatoes, cooked and still hot
½ cup finely chopped onion
1 pound fresh green beans, cooked and still hot

salad dressing
¾ cup vegetable oil
⅓ cup red wine vinegar
¼ teaspoon salt
4 tomatoes, peeled and quartered
4 hard-cooked eggs, quartered
16 large ripe olives
1 small can anchovy fillets (optional)
⅛ teaspoon pepper
¼ teaspoon dry mustard
2 lemons, cut into wedges
1 or 2 7-ounce cans tuna, drained

Slice potatoes into large bowl with a cover. Add onion and green beans.

Mix oil, vinegar, salt, pepper, and mustard.

Pour ⅓ cup dressing over hot vegetables. Cover; let cool to room temperature. Refrigerate for several hours.

To serve salad, place potatoes and green beans on large platter. Carefully arrange tomatoes, eggs, olives, anchovies, lemons, and tuna on platter. Serve dressing separately. Serves 4.

shrimp mousse

2½ pounds fresh shrimp
2 envelopes unflavored gelatin
½ cup cold water
5 hard-boiled eggs
1 small jar stuffed green olives
4 anchovy fillets (optional)
1¼ cups catsup
Grated rind and juice of 2 lemons
1 cup mayonnaise
¼ teaspoon salt

Prepare shrimp according to instructions for Boiled Shrimp.

Soften gelatin in cold water; place over hot water; stir until dissolved. Grind shrimp, eggs, olives and anchovies through a food chopper. Combine catsup, dissolved gelatin, lemon rind and lemon juice; stir in shrimp mixture. Stir in mayonnaise and salt; pour into individual molds or 1 large mold. Chill until firm.

Unmold on salad greens; garnish with additional anchovies and cucumber slices. Serves 6 to 8.

boiled shrimp

2 quarts water
1 tablespoon Worcestershire sauce
⅛ teaspoon hot sauce
10 peppercorns
½ lemon, sliced
2 teaspoons salt
2 bay leaves
1 small onion, halved
1 piece of celery with leaves
3 pounds fresh medium shrimp

Bring water to a boil in a kettle; add remaining ingredients except shrimp. Boil 10 minutes.

Add shrimp; bring to a slow boil; cook, stirring occasionally, 5 minutes. Remove from heat; cover. Let stand 15 minutes. Drain in colander; cool. Peel and devein.

shrimp mousse

jellied fish in tomato juice

1 pound fresh salmon or trout
1 teaspoon salt
6 allspices
2 bay leaves
2 cups water
1½ cups tomato juice
1 bouillon cube
1 package unflavored gelatin

Boil fish, salt, and spices in 2 cups of water until well-done. Cool fish; pick out bones and skin. Flake fish; place in a greased fish mold.

Strain broth; return to stove. Add tomato juice and bouillon; bring broth to a boil. Add gelatin to hot broth; pour it over fish in the mold. Chill until firm and set.

Unmold the jellied fish onto a platter; garnish with parsley. Serves 6.

hamburg-style fish salad

1 tablespoon butter
1 pound whitefish fillets, fresh or frozen (cod, turbot, or haddock)
½ cup hot water
4 hard-cooked eggs
2 dill pickles
1 tablespoon capers

sauce
2 tablespoons mayonnaise
2 tablespoons sour cream
2 teaspoons lemon juice
1 teaspoon dijon-style mustard
½ teaspoon salt
¼ teaspoon white pepper

garnish
1 hard-cooked egg
4 slices canned beets

Melt butter in a frypan. Place fish in frypan; pour hot water over fish. Bring to a boil; cover, lower heat and simmer gently for 10 minutes.

Meanwhile, slice 4 hard-cooked eggs and pickles. Drain fish; cool, and cut into cubes.

Prepare salad sauce by blending mayonnaise, sour cream, lemon juice, mustard, salt, and pepper.

In a separate bowl gently mix fish cubes, egg and pickle slices, and capers. Arrange fish mixture in individual dishes and spoon salad sauce over tops. Chill for 30 minutes.

To garnish, cut remaining egg into eight pieces; chop beet slices. Arrange garnish on each serving. Serve immediately. Serves 4.

hamburg-style fish salad

CASSEROLES AND PIES

fish dumplings with crab sauce

1 pound pike or perch
1 onion
1 tablespoon butter
2 egg whites
1/8 teaspoon cream
1/2 cup bread crumbs
1 teaspoon salt
Dash of pepper
1 tablespoon meat broth

Fillet fish. Peel and dice onion. Cook onion in butter until transparent.

Put fish through a food grinder. Add onion, egg whites, cream, and bread crumbs. Put mixture through food grinder again. Add salt and pepper; form mixture into dumplings.

Place fish dumplings in a greased casserole; add hot meat broth. Cover dish; bake it at 350°F 20 minutes. Serve dumplings warm with Crab Sauce. Serves 6 to 8.

crab sauce

3 tablespoons butter
3 tablespoons flour
Fish broth from dumplings
1 egg yolk
2 tablespoons cream
Salt and pepper to taste
1/4 pound crab meat
1 can green or white asparagus tips
1/2 pound cooked shrimp

Heat butter; add flour, stirring constantly. Add fish broth from the already baked dumplings; let simmer for a few minutes.

Add egg yolk, cream, and salt and pepper to taste. Put in crab meat, asparagus tips, and shrimp. Pour sauce over fish dumplings.

fish dumplings with crab sauce

fish fillets on spinach

1½ pounds fish fillets
Juice of 1 lemon
2 pounds fresh spinach
2 tablespoons vegetable oil
1 medium onion, chopped
1 teaspoon margarine
½ teaspoon salt
⅛ teaspoon white pepper
½ teaspoon grated fresh nutmeg
2 tomatoes, peeled
¼ cup grated mozzarella cheese

Wash fish; pat dry. Sprinkle with lemon juice; let stand 10 minutes. Wash spinach well; chop coarsely.

Heat oil in frypan; add onion; sauté until soft. Fry fish in pan with onions for a few minutes on each side until golden brown. Remove fish and onions; reserve.

Add spinach to frypan; stir-fry 4 to 5 minutes.

Grease casserole dish with margarine. Add spinach. Arrange fish fillets on top of spinach; sprinkle with salt, pepper, and nutmeg. Place peeled and sliced tomatoes on top of fish. Sprinkle with grated cheese. Bake in preheated 350°F oven 15 minutes.
Serves 6.

fish fillets on spinach

japanese-style tuna casserole

1 small can tuna
½ cup diced onion
½ cup diced celery
1 can bean sprouts, rinsed with cold water and drained
¼ cup diced green pepper
Soy sauce to taste

Drain tuna; mix with onion, celery, bean sprouts, green pepper, and soy sauce to taste. Place in casserole; bake at 350°F 30 minutes.

Add additional soy sauce, if needed. Serves 2 to 3.

shrimp with feta cheese

1 tablespoon lemon juice
1¼ pounds medium shrimp, peeled and deveined
2 tablespoons olive oil
¼ cup chopped onion
½ bunch green onions, finely chopped (use only part of the green stems)
1 clove garlic, minced
1 cup tomato puree
¼ cup dry white wine
1 tablespoon butter
1 tablespoon brandy or ouzo
¼ teaspoon oregano
1 tablespoon chopped parsley
¼ pound feta cheese, cut in ½-inch squares

Pour lemon juice over shrimp; let stand while making sauce.

Heat oil in heavy skillet. Add onions (green and white) and garlic; sauté until limp. Add tomato puree and wine; let simmer 15 minutes.

Melt butter; sauté shrimp until pink (3 to 4 minutes).

Gently warm the brandy. Ignite; pour over shrimp. When flame extinguishes, add oregano and parsley.

Transfer the shrimp to small casserole (1½ quart). Take remaining juice from pan in which shrimp were cooked; mix with the tomato-puree sauce. Pour over shrimp. Top with feta cheese; press cheese into sauce. Bake at 375°F for 15 minutes or until hot and bubbly. Serves 4.

oyster soufflé

1 pint standard oysters
3 tablespoons butter
3 tablespoons flour
1 cup half-and-half
1 teaspoon salt
¼ teaspoon white pepper
3 egg yolks, beaten
3 egg whites, beaten stiff

Drain and chop oysters.

Melt butter; blend in flour until a paste forms. Add half-and-half; cook, stirring constantly, until thick. Remove from heat. Add oysters, seasonings, and beaten egg yolks.

Beat egg whites until stiff. Fold into oyster mixture. Pour mixture into greased casserole. Bake in 350°F oven 30 minutes or until brown. Serves 6.

salmon and spaghetti casserole

½ cup butter or margarine
½ cup flour
2 cups hot chicken broth
Salt and pepper
Pinch of nutmeg
¼ cup dry sherry
1 can (about 15 ounces) salmon
¼ cup light cream
2 cups sliced mushrooms
½ pound spaghetti, cooked
½ cup grated Parmesan cheese
½ cup bread or cereal crumbs

Preheat oven to 350°F. Make a sauce with half the butter, flour and chicken broth. Season with salt, pepper and a good pinch of nutmeg.

Add sherry and liquid from the salmon; simmer over low heat 5 minutes. Stir in cream; adjust seasoning. Sauté mushrooms in remaining butter; add to sauce.

Mix half the sauce with cooked spaghetti; put into a shallow casserole. Flake salmon; mix with remaining sauce; pour over spaghetti.

Sprinkle with cheese and bread crumbs mixed together; cook about 20 minutes, or until well browned. Serves 5 to 6.

shad roe casserole with herbs

4 shad roes
2 cups dry white wine
2 cups fish stock or water
1 teaspoon tarragon vinegar
Salt and white pepper
¼ cup warm olive oil
½ cup melted butter
1 teaspoon minced chervil
1 teaspoon minced chives
1 teaspoon minced parsley
1 teaspoon minced rosemary
1 tablespoon chopped shallots
¼ cup sherry

Rinse roes carefully; lay them side by side in a shallow earthenware casserole.

Pour in wine, fish stock or water, and tarragon vinegar; season with salt and white pepper to taste. Bring stock to a boil; simmer roes gently 12 minutes. Drain; reserve stock for another use. Dry roes on a paper towel; brush them with warm olive oil.

Return roes to casserole. Season butter with all minced herbs and shallots; pour seasoned butter over roes. Add sherry.

Do not cover casserole. Braise roes in 350°F oven 10 minutes. Serve in casserole. Serves 4.

company crab

1 pound blue crab meat, pasteurized
1 can (15 ounces) artichoke hearts, drained
1 can (4 ounces) sliced mushrooms, drained
2 tablespoons butter or margarine
2½ tablespoons flour
½ teaspoon salt
Dash of cayenne pepper
1 cup half-and-half cream
2 tablespoons sherry
2 tablespoons cereal crumbs
1 tablespoon grated Parmesan cheese
Paprika

Remove any shell or cartilage from crab meat.

Cut artichoke hearts in half. Place artichokes in a well-greased, shallow 1½-quart casserole. Cover with mushrooms and crab meat.

Melt butter. Blend in flour and seasonings. Add cream gradually; cook until thick, stirring constantly. Stir in sherry. Pour sauce over crab meat.

Combine crumbs and cheese. Sprinkle over sauce. Sprinkle with paprika. Bake in a 450°F oven 12 to 15 minutes or until bubbly. Serves 6.

tuna dinner pie with cheese sauce

2 cans (6½ or 7 ounces each) tuna
½ cup chopped onion
2 tablespoons margarine or cooking oil
2 tablespoons flour
½ teaspoon salt
Dash of pepper
1½ cups undiluted evaporated milk
2 eggs, beaten
9-inch unbaked pastry shell
Cheese Sauce
Tomato slices, optional

Drain and flake tuna. Cook onion in saucepan in margarine or oil until tender, but not brown. Stir in flour, salt and pepper. Add milk; cook, stirring constantly, until thickened. Pour mixture over eggs very slowly, beating constantly.

Bake crust in moderate oven, 375°F, about 5 minutes. Remove crust from oven and spread tuna over crust; pour egg mixture over tuna. Return pie to oven; bake about 25 to 30 minutes or until filling is set.

Let stand about 10 minutes before cutting into wedges. Serve with Cheese Sauce. Garnish with thin tomato slices, if desired. Makes one 9-inch pie, 4 to 6 servings.

cheese sauce

1 can (10¾ ounce) condensed cheddar cheese soup
½ cup undiluted evaporated milk

Combine soup and milk in saucepan; heat, stirring, until hot and smooth. Makes about 1¾ cups sauce.

pilgrims clam pie

3 dozen shell clams
or
3 cans (8 ounces each) minced clams
1½ cups water
¼ cup margarine or butter
½ cup sliced fresh mushrooms
2 tablespoons minced onion
¼ cup all-purpose flour
¼ teaspoon dry mustard
⅛ teaspoon liquid hot pepper sauce
¼ teaspoon salt
⅛ teaspoon white pepper
1 cup reserved clam liquor
1 cup half-and-half
1 tablespoon lemon juice
2 tablespoons chopped parsley
2 tablespoons chopped pimento
Pastry for a 1-crust 9-inch pie
1 egg, beaten

Wash clam shells thoroughly. Place clams in a large pot with water. Bring to a boil; simmer 8 to 10 minutes or until clams open. Remove clams from shells; cut into fourths. Reserve 1 cup clam liquor. (If using canned clams, drain and reserve 1 cup liquor).

In a skillet melt margarine. Add mushrooms and onion; cook until tender. Stir in flour, mustard, liquid hot pepper sauce, salt, and pepper. Gradually add clam liquor and half-and-half. Cook, stirring constantly, until thick. Stir in lemon juice, parsley, pimento, and clams.

Pour mixture into a 9-inch-round deep-dish pie plate (about 2 inches deep). Roll out pastry dough; place on top of mixture in pie plate; secure dough to rim of pie plate by crimping. Vent pastry. Brush with beaten egg. Bake in a 375°F oven 25 to 30 minutes or until pastry is browned. Serves 6.

crab cheese pie

6 to 8 ounces Alaska snow crab, frozen or canned
1½ cups Jack cheese, grated
2 eggs, beaten
½ cup milk
2 tablespoons green onion, minced
8-ounce can refrigerated crescent rolls

Drain and slice crab. Combine with cheese, eggs, milk and onion.

Line a 9-inch pie plate with 5 triangles of crescent roll dough. Press together to form a crust.

Spoon in crab mixture. Top with remaining triangles. Bake in a 325°F oven 50 to 60 minutes. Serves 5 to 6.

MAIN DISHES

poached haddock with mussels

2 pounds haddock, cod, or other thick fillets, fresh or frozen
4 pounds mussels in shells (about 4 dozen) or clams may be substituted
1 cup dry white wine
1 cup water
1 small onion, sliced
½ teaspoon salt
½ cup whipping cream
¼ cup margarine or butter
Dash of white pepper
Dash of nutmeg
2 tablespoons chopped parsley
Parslied potatoes
1 cup each of zucchini, carrots, and celery, cut julienne style
Margarine or butter for cooking vegetables

Thaw fillets if frozen. Cut into serving-size portions.

Clean mussels in cold water. Scrub shells with a stiff brush, rinsing thoroughly several times.

Combine wine, water, and onion in large pan; bring to simmering stage. Add cleaned mussels. Cover; steam about 5 minutes or until shells open. Remove mussels from shells; set aside.

Strain cooking liquid into a large skillet. Add fillets and salt. Cover; simmer 8 to 10 minutes or until fish flakes easily. Transfer fillets to warm platter; keep warm.

Reduce cooking liquid to ½ cup. Stir in whipping cream, ¼ cup margarine or butter, pepper, and nutmeg; simmer until sauce thickens slightly. Add mussels and parsley; heat. Spoon mixture over fillets.

Serve with parslied potatoes and julienne strips of zucchini, carrots, and celery sautéed in margarine or butter, stirring constantly just until tender. Serves 6.

seafood newburg

seafood newburg

4 tablespoons butter or margarine
4 cups fresh or frozen uncooked seafood (lobster, shrimp, crab meat, or fish fillets, all in 1-inch pieces)
3 tablespoons lemon juice
1 tablespoon flour
1 teaspoon salt
½ teaspoon paprika
⅛ teaspoon cayenne pepper
2 cups light cream
3 egg yolks
2 tablespoons sherry
6 cups hot cooked rice
Parsley for garnish

Melt butter in large skillet. Sauté seafood about 5 minutes, stirring constantly. Sprinkle with lemon juice.

Mix flour, salt, paprika, and pepper; add to seafood. Remove from heat. Gradually stir in 1½ cups of cream. Return to heat until sauce comes to simmer.

Combine egg yolks with remaining ½ cup cream; blend ¼ cup hot liquid mixture with this. Return this to skillet; stir until slightly thickened. Add sherry last, and liberally if you prefer.

Serve over rice, garnished with parsley. Serves 6 to 8.

seafood linguine

¼ pound butter or margarine
2 cans minced clams, drained
1 clove garlic, minced fine
1 teaspoon salt
¼ teaspoon pepper
½ pound shrimp, cooked and deveined
2 teaspoons lemon juice
1 pound linguine, cooked

Melt butter in medium skillet. Add all ingredients (except linguine) in order given. Cook on low heat 15 minutes, stirring occasionally. Pour over linguine; serve. Serves 4 to 6.

chipper perch

2 pounds yellow perch fillets or other fish fillets, fresh or frozen
½ cup Caesar salad dressing
1 cup crushed potato chips
½ cup shredded sharp cheddar cheese

Thaw fillets. Dip fillets in salad dressing. Place fillets in a single layer, skin-side-down, on a baking pan, 15 × 10 × 1 inches.

Combine crushed chips and cheese. Sprinkle over fillets. Bake in an extremely hot oven, 500°F, 10 to 15 minutes or until fillets flake easily. Serves 6.

baked fish

1 pound fish fillets (sole, flounder, or red snapper)
1 tablespoon chopped parsley
1 tablespoon lemon juice
¾ teaspoon seasoned salt
3 tablespoons olive oil
1 medium onion, thinly sliced
1 clove garlic, minced
1 large tomato, chopped
3 slices lemon
2 tablespoons white wine

Arrange fish in an 8- or 9-inch-square baking dish. Sprinkle with parsley, lemon juice, and seasoned salt.

Heat the oil in a small skillet; fry onion and garlic until limp.

Top fish with onion mixture, including oil from skillet. Arrange tomatoes on top of onion mixture; place lemon slices on top of fish. Pour wine over all; bake at 350°F 30 to 35 minutes or until fish flakes with a fork. Serves 3.

baked fish

fish fillets india

fish fillets india

1/2 cup flour
2 teaspoons curry powder
1/4 teaspoon salt
1 pound fresh or frozen fillets (your choice of favorite fish)
1/2 cup margarine
1/2 cup chopped blanched almonds
Chutney

Mix flour, curry powder, and salt well. Thoroughly coat each piece of fish with this mixture.

Heat margarine in a large skillet. Brown fish over moderate heat, about 4 minutes per side. When fish flakes easily, it is done through. Remove fillets; place on a heated serving dish. Add almonds to shortening left in skillet; stir until nuts are browned. Pour over fish. Serve the chutney as a relish. Serves 4.

quick and easy creamed tuna

1 package cream of celery soup (can substitute cream of chicken or cream of mushroom soup)
2 cups water
1 6 1/2-ounce can tuna, drained
3 tablespoons chopped onion

Heat dry soup with water; add tuna and onion. Heat through, adding more water if mixture becomes too thick.

Delicious over baking powder biscuits, toast points, rice, noodles or scones. Serves 3.

fast fish broil

2 pounds skinless catfish fillets or other fish fillets, fresh or frozen
1/4 cup garlic French dressing
3 tablespoons soy sauce
3/4 teaspoon ground ginger
Lime slices

Thaw frozen fillets. Place fillets in a single layer, skinned-side-down, on a bake-and-serve platter, 16 × 10 inches.

Combine French dressing, soy sauce, and ginger. Pour sauce over fillets; let stand 10 minutes. Broil about 4 inches from source of heat 10 to 15 minutes or until fillets flake easily when tested with a fork. Baste once during broiling with sauce in pan.

Garnish with lime slices. Serves 6.

japanese fish

1 whole trout, about 1 pound
1 whole carp, about 3 pounds
Juice of 1 lemon
Salt
White pepper
2 slices lean bacon
Margarine to grease pan
4 large leaves savoy cabbage (if unavailable, use regular cabbage)
1 pound fresh mushrooms
2 pieces sugared or candied ginger
3 tablespoons soy sauce
Pinch of ground anise
1 cup hot water
2 teaspoons cornstarch
Cold water
2 tablespoons bacon drippings
Juice of 1/2 lemon

garnish
2 tablespoons chopped parsley
Lemon slices

Scale and clean out the insides of fish, but leave fish whole.

Wash fish thoroughly under running water; pat dry; rub with lemon juice. With sharp knife make shallow incisions in backs of both fish; rub with salt and pepper. Cut bacon into small strips; insert one strip in each incision.

Grease ovenproof baking dish with margarine; line with cabbage leaves. Place fish on top. Slice mushrooms and sugared ginger. Mix together; spoon over fish. Sprinkle with soy sauce and ground anise. Pour in small amount of hot water. Cover with lid or aluminum foil; place in preheated 350°F oven. Bake 30 minutes. While baking, gradually add rest of hot water; baste fish with pan drippings. Remove fish and cabbage leaves from pan. Arrange on a preheated platter.

Bring pan drippings to a boil, scraping all brown particles from bottom of pan and adding more water, if necessary. Blend cornstarch with small amount of cold water; add to pan drippings; stir until sauce is smooth and bubbly. Correct seasonings; serve separately.

Melt and heat bacon drippings. Pour over fish; sprinkle with lemon juice. Garnish fish with chopped parsley and lemon slices.
Serves 4.

baked fish with mushroom stuffing

mushroom stuffing
3 tablespoons butter
1 small onion, chopped
½ cup chopped fresh mushrooms
2 cups dry bread crumbs
¾ cup chicken stock
1 egg, beaten
½ teaspoon salt
¼ teaspoon pepper

4-pound whole fish of your choice, dressed
1 teaspoon salt
4 strips bacon

Prepare Mushroom Stuffing. Put butter in saucepan. Add onion; sauté until onion is golden but not brown. Add chopped mushrooms; cook until water from mushrooms cooks away. Remove from heat. Add bread crumbs, chicken stock, egg, ½ teaspoon salt, and pepper. Mix well with your hands.

Clean and rub inside of fish with 1 teaspoon salt. Stuff fish. Fasten with toothpicks. Place fish, underside down, in greased baking dish. Layer bacon over top of fish. Bake in 350°F oven 1 hour or until fish flakes easily with a fork.

Remove fish to a hot platter to serve. Serves 8.

fish cakes

1 egg
1 tablespoon lemon juice
1 onion, minced fine
2 tablespoons prepared mustard
½ teaspoon salt
¼ teaspoon pepper
1 teaspoon parsley flakes
1 pound cooked fish, boned and flaked
¼ cup corn flake crumbs (at least)
Fat for deep frying

Mix egg, lemon juice, onion, and seasonings in a bowl. Toss with flaked fish. Add enough corn flake crumbs to allow you to shape fish cakes easily. Roll each cake in extra crumbs to coat the outside.

Heat fat in medium skillet; fry cakes until crisp and brown on the outside. Drain on paper towels; place on a heated platter. Serves 4 to 6.

clam sauce supreme

2 tablespoons butter or margarine
1 tablespoon flour
1 teaspoon garlic salt
2 8-ounce cans minced clams with liquid
1 teaspoon parsley
1 teaspoon salt
½ teaspoon pepper
Cooked thin spaghetti

In medium skillet melt butter on low heat. Stir in flour and garlic salt, using a wire whisk. Add juice from canned clams; continue to stir. Add seasonings and, last, the clams. Simmer 10 minutes. Pour over cooked thin spaghetti. Serves 4 to 6.

sherry delight

1½ pounds haddock fish fillets
¼ cup flour
¼ cup oil
½ teaspoon sugar
½ teaspoon ginger
¼ teaspoon garlic powder
1 tablespoon soy sauce
1 tablespoon sherry
Water
½ teaspoon freshly ground black pepper
¼ cup chives or ends of spring onions
1 tablespoon parsley
2 medium-size tomatoes, chopped
1 teaspoon cornstarch
Salt to taste
½ cup water or sherry

Coat fillets with flour. Heat oil in skillet; brown fish on both sides.

Combine sugar, ginger, garlic, soy sauce, sherry, and water to make 1 cup. Pour over fish. Cover skillet; simmer 10 minutes. Add black pepper, chives, parsley, and tomatoes. Cook uncovered 5 minutes.

Mix together cornstarch, salt, and ½ cup water or sherry. Blend well; add to fish. Simmer uncovered 5 minutes more. Sauce will thicken slightly and smell heavenly. Serves 4.

fish kabobs

¼ cup olive oil
¼ cup dry white wine
¼ cup lemon juice
2 cloves garlic, minced
3 bay leaves
½ teaspoon dried oregano
½ teaspoon salt
¼ teaspoon pepper
1¼ to 1½ pounds swordfish or halibut steak
2 red peppers, cut in chunks
2 green peppers, cut in chunks
1 onion, cut in wedges
Paprika

the day before serving

Combine oil, wine, lemon juice, garlic, bay leaves, oregano, salt, and pepper.

Cut fish into 1½-inch squares; add to marinade. Cover; marinate in refrigerator overnight.

to cook

Alternate fish, peppers, and onions on thin skewers. Dust with paprika and broil approximately 10 minutes. (May also be charcoal-grilled.)

cocktail sauce

1 cup tomato catsup
½ teaspoon dry mustard
2 tablespoons horseradish

Combine the catsup, dry mustard, and horseradish. Mix to combine well; let stand a few minutes before serving.

Serve the kabobs on a bed of rice and pass the Cocktail Sauce. Serves 4.

faster flounder

2 pounds skinless flounder fillets or other fish fillets, fresh or frozen
2 tablespoons grated onion
1½ teaspoons salt
⅛ teaspoon pepper
2 large tomatoes, cut into small pieces
¼ cup butter or margarine, melted
1 cup shredded Swiss cheese

Thaw frozen fillets. Place fillets in a single layer on a well-greased 16- × 10-inch platter.

Sprinkle fillets with onion, salt, and pepper. Cover fillets with tomatoes. Pour butter over tomatoes. Broil about 4 inches from source of heat 10 to 12 minutes or until fillets flake easily.

Remove from heat; sprinkle with cheese. Broil 2 to 3 minutes longer or until cheese melts. Serves 6.

fish teriyaki

marinade
1 cup soy sauce
¼ cup sugar (a little more, if you prefer it sweeter)
¼ cup salad oil
2 teaspoons grated fresh gingerroot or ground ginger
1 large clove of garlic, chopped fine

1½ to 2 pounds fish fillets (rock, red snapper, ocean perch, or haddock)
1 tablespoon sesame seeds

Combine soy sauce, sugar, oil, ginger, and garlic in a bowl.

Let fish fillets marinate in marinade 3 to 4 hours. After arranging fish on broiling pan, pour on a little marinade. Broil 6 inches from heat about 4 minutes. Turn, add a little more marinade; sprinkle fish with sesame seeds. Broil about 4 minutes longer, or until fish flakes. Serves 4.

marinated fish

1¼ pounds rockfish, red snapper, or sole fillets
½ cup all-purpose flour
½ teaspoon salt
¼ teaspoon pepper
4 tablespoons olive oil
2 cloves garlic, finely chopped
4 tablespoons wine vinegar
½ teaspoon rosemary

Thaw fish if frozen. Combine flour, salt, and pepper; dredge fish fillets, coating well. Shake off excess flour.

Heat oil in a large skillet. Fry fish fillets, a few at a time, until golden brown. Drain on paper towels; keep warm.

When all fish has been cooked, add garlic, vinegar, and rosemary. Stir, scraping up browned bits in pan. Cook for a few minutes; pour over fish on a platter. Serve fish warm or cold. Serves 4.

italian scampi

2 pounds raw clams
2 cloves garlic, minced
1/4 cup butter
1/4 cup oil
1 teaspoon salt
1 tablespoon lemon juice

Remove clams from shell; clean. In a pan sauté garlic for 3 minutes in butter mixed with oil; add salt; stir in lemon juice. Stir-fry clams in mixture about 5 minutes. Serves 4.

fish with lemon sauce

1 1/2 pounds fish fillets
Juice of 1 lemon
2 medium onions, chopped
2 tablespoons vegetable oil
1/2 teaspoon salt
1/8 teaspoon white pepper
1/2 cup water
2 thin slices fresh gingerroot
1/4 teaspoon mace
Grated rind of 1 lemon
1/4 cup lemon juice
1 tablespoon cornstarch
1/4 cup water
1/4 teaspoon saffron
1/4 cup plain yogurt
Chopped parsley for garnish

Wash fish; pat dry. Sprinkle with juice of 1 lemon; let stand for 10 minutes.

Sauté onions in hot oil until golden brown. Add fish; brown on both sides about 5 minutes. Add salt, pepper, water, gingerroot, mace, lemon rind, and lemon juice. Simmer, covered, 10 minutes. Remove fish; keep warm.

Mix cornstarch with water; stir in fish sauce. Add saffron; simmer sauce 2 minutes to thicken. Stir in yogurt; remove from heat; garnish and serve immediately. Serves 4.

fish with lemon sauce

fish steaks with shrimp sauce

4 fish steaks (each 6 to 8 ounces)
Juice of 1 lemon
½ teaspoon salt
¼ teaspoon white pepper
2 tablespoons margarine
1 medium onion, sliced
1 tablespoon chopped parsley
½ cup dry white wine
½ cup beef bouillon
6 ounces fresh mushrooms, sliced
¼ pound frozen cooked shrimps
1 tablespoon lemon juice
¼ cup plain yogurt
Lemon slices and parsley for garnish

Wash fish; pat dry; sprinkle with juice of 1 lemon, salt, and pepper.

Heat margarine in a frypan; add fish and onion; brown fish 5 minutes on each side. Sprinkle with parsley; pour in white wine; simmer 5 minutes. Remove fish to a heated platter; keep warm.

Add bouillon to frypan; bring to boil. Add mushrooms; simmer slowly 8 minutes, stirring often. Add shrimps; simmer 2 to 3 minutes. Season sauce with 1 tablespoon lemon juice, and stir in yogurt. Heat thoroughly, but do not boil. Adjust seasonings.

Pour over fish steaks; garnish with lemon slices and parsley. Serves 4.

fish steaks with shrimp sauce

steamed whole fish

1½ pounds whole fish (flounder, pike, trout, or sea bass)
1 teaspoon salt
½ teaspoon freshly ground pepper
¼ teaspoon powdered ginger
3 cups water
2 teaspoons mixed pickling spices (more, if you prefer it spicier)
2 bay leaves
2 cloves garlic, cut in half
2 tablespoons chopped scallion

garnish
Lemon slices
Tomato
Parsley

Have fish scaled and cleaned and head removed, if you prefer. Lightly score skin so seasonings will flavor fish.

Combine salt, pepper, and ginger; rub on fish thoroughly.

Pour water into large frying pan or wok; add pickling spices, bay leaves, garlic, and scallion. Place rack in pan so fish will sit above liquid, in order to allow steam to circulate. Place fish on rack; cover; simmer approximately 30 minutes, or until fish is tender.

Garnish fish with lemon slices, tomato, and parsley. Serves 3.

steamed whole fish

baked halibut

1 slice halibut, about 2 inches thick
3 tablespoons butter
1 teaspoon salt
Dash of freshly ground pepper
1 cup canned tomatoes
½ teaspoon sugar
½ medium-size onion
½ cup heavy cream

Pat halibut dry on paper towels. Remove skin. Put fish in a buttered baking dish; sprinkle it with salt and pepper. Brush remaining butter over fish. Add tomatoes crushed with sugar. Cover with thinly sliced onion.

Bake fish 20 minutes at 400°F; pour cream over it; bake 10 minutes more. Serves 4 or more.

deep-fried scallops with sweet-and-sour sauce

batter

1 cup sifted all-purpose flour
3/4 cup water
1 large egg
1/2 teaspoon salt
2 cups oil for frying

1 pound scallops (cubed fish fillets may be substituted)

sweet-and-sour sauce

4 pineapple rings, cut into small pieces
Reserved pineapple syrup and water to make 1 cup
1 tablespoon cornstarch in 2 tablespoons cold water
2 tablespoons vinegar
1/4 cup brown sugar
1 teaspoon soy sauce
1 small onion, sliced
Few strips each of carrots and green pepper

2 cups hot boiled rice

Combine batter ingredients; beat just until smooth. Allow to stand 1 hour. Dip scallops, a few at a time, into batter; deep-fry in oil at 375°F just until golden brown and done, about 3 to 4 minutes. Drain on paper towels.

Combine sauce ingredients in a saucepan. Stir constantly while bringing to a boil. Heat until thickened and carrot and pepper strips are heated through.

Place scallops on a bed of boiled rice; cover with sauce. Serve at once while scallop batter coating is still crisp. Serves 4.

fried trout grenoble

4 freshwater trout, fresh or frozen (each about 1/2 pound)
Juice of 1 lemon
Salt
5 tablespoons flour
1/2 cup vegetable oil
1/4 cup butter
1 slice dry bread, crumbled
2 tablespoons capers
1 lemon, sliced
Parsley sprigs for garnish

Thoroughly wash fish; pat dry with paper towels. Sprinkle with half the lemon juice; let stand 5 minutes. Salt trout inside and out; roll in flour.

Heat oil in frypan. Add trout; fry 5 minutes on each side or until golden. Remove fish carefully with slotted spoon; discard oil. Melt butter in same frypan. Return trout to pan; fry 5 minutes on each side. Remove; arrange on preheated platter.

Add bread crumbs to butter; cook until browned. Pour over trout. Sprinkle rest of lemon juice over trout. Top with drained capers. Garnish with lemon slices and parsley sprigs. Serves 4.

fried-trout grenoble

blue trout

4 ¾-pound freshwater trout (eviscerated only)
2 teaspoons salt
1 cup vinegar, heated
4 cups water
¼ cup white wine
1 sprig parsley for garnish
1 lemon for garnish
1 tomato for garnish

Rinse fish thoroughly with cold water. Sprinkle ¼ teaspoon salt inside each fish. To make trout look attractive, tie a thread through tail and underside of mouth to form a ring. Arrange fish on a large platter; pour hot vinegar over them. This process will turn them blue in color.

In a 4-quart saucepot bring water, remaining salt, and wine to a simmer. Carefully place trout in water; simmer (be sure not to boil) about 15 minutes. Remove trout with a slotted spoon; drain on paper towels; arrange on a preheated platter. Garnish with parsley, lemon, and tomato slices. Serves 4.

fisherman's trout

4 (approximately 8-inch) brook trout
Flour seasoned with lemon pepper
¼ cup butter or margarine
3 tablespoons more butter or margarine
Lemon wedges

Clean and wash trout, cutting off fins. Leave heads and tails on or not, as desired. Dip cleaned trout in seasoned flour.

Melt ¼ cup butter in a large skillet; sauté trout until tender and browned on both sides. Remove to a hot platter.

Add remaining 3 tablespoons of butter to skillet; allow it to brown. Pour over fish. Serve fish with lemon wedges. Serves 4.

michigan pickled lake trout

2 pounds lake trout fillets or other fish fillets, fresh or frozen
2 tablespoons margarine or butter
½ cup minced onion
1½ cups apple juice
1 cup cider vinegar
⅔ cup firmly packed light brown sugar
½ cup seedless raisins
2 bay leaves
1 teaspoon salt
½ cup crushed gingersnaps

Thaw fillets if frozen. Cut into serving size portions.

In a skillet melt margarine. Add onion; cook until tender. Stir in apple juice, vinegar, brown sugar, raisins, bay leaves, and salt. Heat to boiling; simmer 5 minutes to blend flavors.

Add fish fillets; cover and simmer 3 to 5 minutes or until fish flakes easily. Remove fish to serving dish. Gradually add gingersnaps to poaching liquid, stirring until smooth and thickened. Serve over fish. Serves 6.

crispy fried rainbow trout

6 pan-dressed rainbow trout or other small fish, fresh or frozen
¼ cup evaporated milk
1½ teaspoons salt
Dash of pepper
½ cup flour
¼ cup yellow cornmeal
1 teaspoon paprika
12 slices bacon

Thaw fish. Clean, wash, and dry fish.

Combine milk, salt, and pepper. Combine flour, cornmeal, and paprika. Dip fish in milk mixture and roll in flour mixture.

Fry bacon in a heavy frypan until crisp. Remove bacon, reserving fat for frying. Drain bacon on absorbent paper.

Fry fish in hot fat for 4 minutes. Turn carefully; fry 4 to 6 minutes longer or until fish is brown and flakes easily when tested with a fork. Drain on abosrbent paper. Serve with bacon. Serves 6.

breezy salmon bake

2 pounds salmon steaks or other fish steaks, fresh or frozen
2 tablespoons grated onion
1¼ teaspoons dillweed
1 teaspoon salt
Dash of pepper
1 tablespoon butter or margarine
¾ cup light cream

Place thawed steaks in a single layer in a well-greased baking dish, 12 × 8 × 2 inches.

Sprinkle steaks with onion, dillweed, salt, and pepper. Dot with butter.

Pour cream over steaks. Bake in 350°F oven 25 to 30 minutes or until steaks flake easily. Serves 6.

spanish-style turbot

4 turbot fillets (4 to 6 ounces each)
1 lemon, juiced
½ teaspoon salt
2 tablespoons flour
2 tablespoons margarine
1 onion, chopped
1 green pepper, cut in ½-inch cubes
1 clove garlic, minced
½ teaspoon paprika
2 small tomatoes, peeled and cut in quarters
¼ teaspoon white pepper
¼ teaspoon saffron
¼ teaspoon ground nutmeg
½ cup dry white wine
2 sprigs parsley, chopped

Wash and dry fish fillets with paper towels. Sprinkle with lemon juice; let fish stand 5 to 10 minutes. Salt fish; dip each fillet into flour to coat.

Heat margarine in a large frypan; lightly brown fish on each side about 3 minutes. Remove; keep warm.

Sauté onion, green pepper, and garlic in remaining hot margarine. After 2 minutes, add paprika and tomatoes. Season with pepper, saffron, and nutmeg. Add white wine; return fish fillets to pan. Cover; gently simmer 15 minutes. Place fish fillets on a preheated platter. Pour sauce over fish; sprinkle with chopped parsley. Serves 4.

buffet tuna and noodles

½ cup butter or margarine
2 large cloves garlic, minced
1 cup coarsely chopped red pepper
½ cup finely chopped onion
2 tablespoons flour
1½ cups chicken broth, or vegetable cooking liquid
¼ cup chopped parsley
1 can (5¾ ounces) pitted ripe olives, sliced
2 cans (6½ or 7 ounces each) tuna in vegetable oil, flaked
1 package (8 ounces) spinach-egg noodles
1 tablespoon salad oil

In large skillet melt butter over medium heat; stir in garlic. Add red pepper and onion; sauté until tender. Blend in flour; cook 1 minute. Add chicken broth, parsley and olives. Cook, stirring constantly, until sauce thickens. Stir in tuna.

Cook noodles according to package directions, adding 1 tablespoon salad oil to cooking water. Drain noodles; turn into large, heated serving dish. Spoon tuna sauce over noodles.

Serve with all or several of the following sprinkles: chopped walnuts, crushed corn chips, grated Parmesan cheese, sieved hard-cooked egg, cooked green peas. Serves 4 to 6.

creamy tuna-topped broccoli

1 bunch fresh broccoli
4 tablespoons butter or margarine
½ cup finely chopped celery
½ cup finely chopped onion
2 tablespoons flour
1½ cups milk
1 teaspoon Worcestershire sauce
½ cup shredded processed American cheese
2 cans (6½ or 7 ounces each) tuna, drained of excess liquid and flaked

Wash broccoli; remove large leaves and tough part of stalks. Cut stalks lengthwise into quarters.

Place broccoli in large saucepan with 1-inch boiling, salted water. Cover; cook 10 to 12 minutes, until crisp-tender. Drain broccoli well; reserve cooking water.

In large saucepan, melt butter over medium heat; sauté celery and onion until soft. Stir in flour, blending well. Combine reserved cooking water and milk; gradually stir into saucepan; cook, stirring, until mixture is slightly thickened and comes to boiling.

Add Worcestershire sauce and cheese; stir until cheese is melted. Stir in tuna; heat through. Serve hot over cooked broccoli. Serves 4.

steamed haddock with mediterranean sauce

steamed haddock with mediterranean sauce

6 medium tomatoes
1/2 teaspoon dried oregano
1/2 teaspoon thyme
1/2 teaspoon basil
1 teaspoon chives
2 green onions, finely minced
1/3 cup vermouth
2 pounds haddock or cod fillets
Salt and freshly ground pepper to taste
1 tablespoon olive oil

Peel tomatoes; chop coarsely. Combine tomatoes, herbs, green onions and vermouth in a medium-sized saucepan. Simmer for 30 minutes while preparing haddock.

Place haddock on a large piece of aluminum foil. Season with salt and pepper. Fold foil around haddock securely. Place haddock in a steamer over boiling water. Steam about 20 minutes or until fish begins to flake.

Pour juice from foil packet into tomato sauce. Rewrap foil packet; keep haddock warm in a very slow oven.

Add olive oil to sauce; simmer about 30 minutes longer or until thickened and considerably reduced in volume. Arrange haddock on a heated platter. Pour sauce over haddock; serve. Serves 5 to 6.

key lime mullet

2 pounds mullet fillets or other fish fillets, fresh or frozen
1 teaspoon salt
Dash of pepper
¼ cup lime juice
3 tablespoons butter or margarine, melted
Paprika
Lime wedges

Thaw frozen fillets. Skin fillets; cut into serving-size portions. Place fish in a single layer in a shallow baking dish. Sprinkle with salt and pepper.

Pour lime juice over fish; let stand 30 minutes, turning once. Remove fish, reserving juice.

Place fish on a well-greased broiler pan. Combine butter and juice. Brush fish with butter mixture; sprinkle with paprika.

Broil about 4 inches from source of heat 8 to 10 minutes or until fish flakes easily when tested with a fork. Serve with lime wedges. Serves 6.

fish veracruz style

2 pounds black bass or other fish, boned
Lemon juice to taste
3 to 4 small fresh tomatoes (1 pound), sliced
2 green chili peppers, sliced
1 onion, sliced
Salt and pepper to taste
Oregano to taste
1 tablespoon vinegar
1 tablespoon olive oil or salad oil
3 bay leaves
2 tablespoons melted fat (margarine or butter)

Put half the fish in a baking pan or dish. Sprinkle with lemon juice.

Add a layer of half the tomatoes, chilies, onion, salt, pepper, and oregano. Repeat layers.

Mix vinegar, oil, bay leaves, and fat. Pour over fish. Bake at 350°F until fish is tender. Serves 6.

coddies

3 medium potatoes, cooked and mashed
¼ pound butter or margarine
3 eggs, beaten
1 medium onion, chopped fine
1 teaspoon salt
¼ teaspoon pepper
1 tablespoon chopped parsley
3 15-ounce cans codfish
Fat for deep frying

Mash potatoes smooth; add butter while potatoes are still hot. Add beaten eggs, onion, salt, pepper, parsley, and codfish. Mix well; let stand at least 1 hour.

Shape coddies into 2-inch cakes.

Heat fat in medium-size skillet. Fry coddies until brown and crisp. Drain on paper towels. Serves 4 to 6.

crusted herring

crusted herring

8 green herring
2 tablespoons lemon juice
1 teaspoon salt
3 tablespoons fine herbs
2 tablespoons bread crumbs
Parmesan cheese
4 tablespoons butter

Fillet herring carefully; wash; let dry. Cover with lemon juice; set aside 10 minutes.

Put herring in a greased baking dish; sprinkle with salt and fine herbs. Spread bread crumbs and Parmesan cheese over that. Melt butter; pour over fish.

Bake fish 20 minutes at 425°F. Serve hot. Serves 4 to 6.

shrimp, lobster, and crab diavolo

1¼-pound live lobster
1 pound king crab legs
2 pounds medium shrimp, raw
½ cup butter
2 tablespoons olive oil
2 cloves garlic, peeled and minced
⅛ teaspoon crushed red pepper
Juice of 1 lemon
2 tablespoons chopped parsley

Steam lobster and crab legs; cool. Peel shrimp, leaving tails intact. Butterfly and remove sand vein. Drain well. Remove lobster and crab from shells; slice.

In a large heavy skillet, heat butter and oil over moderate heat. Add garlic and sauté 2 minutes. Add shrimp and pepper; sauté until shrimp turns pink. Add crab and lobster; heat through.

Sprinkle with lemon juice and parsley; serve with garlic bread. Serves 4 to 5.

crab cakes

1 pound crab meat
1 egg yolk
1½ teaspoons salt
Healthy dash of black pepper
1 teaspoon dry mustard
2 teaspoons Worcestershire sauce
1 tablespoon mayonnaise
1 tablespoon chopped parsley
½ teaspoon paprika
1 tablespoon melted butter
Bread crumbs for coating cakes
Liquid shortening for frying

Lightly toss crab meat and all ingredients (except bread crumbs) in order listed. When well-blended, shape into cakes. Roll each cake in bread crumbs until coated on all sides.

Heat shortening in skillet. Fry crab cakes quickly in hot fat until golden brown. Serves 4 to 6.

crab cakes

imperial crab

1 green sweet pepper, minced
1 medium onion, minced
2 teaspoons dry mustard
2 teaspoons prepared horseradish
2 teaspoons salt
½ teaspoon freshly ground white pepper
2 eggs, beaten
1 cup mayonnaise
3 pounds lump crab meat
Paprika

Combine green pepper, onion, mustard, horseradish, salt, white pepper and eggs; mix well. Blend in mayonnaise thoroughly; fold in crab meat.

Spoon crab meat mixture into 8 large cleaned crab shells or ramekins. Coat with additional mayonnaise; sprinkle generously with paprika.

Arrange crab shells in a shallow oblong baking pan. Bake in a preheated 350°F oven 15 to 20 minutes or until heated through. Serves 8.

snappy snapper

2 pounds skinless snapper fillets or other fish fillets, fresh or frozen
½ cup frozen orange juice concentrate, thawed
¼ cup salad oil
¼ cup soy sauce
¼ cup cider vinegar
½ teaspoon salt
Chopped parsley

Thaw frozen fillets. Cut fillets into 6 portions. Place fish in a single layer, skin-side-up, on a well-greased baking pan.

Combine remaining ingredients except parsley. Brush fish with sauce.

Broil about 4 inches from source of heat for 5 minutes. Turn fish carefully; brush with sauce. Broil 5 to 7 minutes longer or until lightly browned and fish flakes easily when tested with a fork. Sprinkle with parsley. Serves 6.

seafood supreme

2 pounds fresh or frozen shrimp, cooked
12 ounces crab meat, fresh or frozen
1 can (6½ ounces) lobster
1 cup butter or margarine
1¼ cups flour
5 cups milk
1 cup sherry
¾ tablespoon salt
½ teaspoon white pepper
1 tablespoon Worcestershire sauce
½ teaspoon dry mustard
¾ pound (3 cups) mild cheddar cheese, grated
1 pound fresh mushrooms, sliced
¼ cup margarine
1 can (4 ounces) pimento, chopped
Patty shells, rice or toast points

Defrost shrimp and crab meat if frozen. Drain canned lobster. Melt butter; blend in flour. Gradually add milk and ½ cup sherry. Cook, stirring constantly, until thick. Add seasonings and cheese; cook, stirring, until cheese is melted and blended into sauce. May be cooled and refrigerated at this point.

Before serving, sauté mushrooms in ¼ cup margarine. Combine and heat sauce with seafood, mushrooms and pimento. Blend in the remaining sherry; serve over toast points, patty shells or rice. Serves 12.

opulent oysters

3 cans (8 ounces each) oysters
1 can (3½ ounces) French fried onions
¼ cup light cream
2 tablespoons grated Parmesan cheese
2 tablespoons butter or margarine

Drain oysters thoroughly. Spread ¾ cup of onions in a well-greased round baking dish, 8 × 2 inches. Cover with oysters. Pour cream over oysters.

Combine remaining onions and cheese. Sprinkle over top. Dot with butter. Bake in 450°F oven 8 to 10 minutes or until lightly browned. Serves 6.

stuffed fillets of sole

shrimp stuffing

2 tablespoons minced shallots or green onions
2 tablespoons butter or margarine
½ pound mushrooms, sliced
2 tablespoons chopped parsley
½ pound tiny shrimp, cooked and cleaned

6 fillets of sole
2 tablespoons butter
2 tablespoons flour
1 cup dry white wine
½ cup heavy cream or half-and-half
¼ teaspoon salt
2 tablespoons brandy
½ cup grated Swiss cheese

Cook shallots in 2 tablespoons melted butter until transparent. Add mushrooms; cook until all liquid has evaporated. Add parsley and shrimp.

Place about 2 tablespoons stuffing on large end of each fillet. Roll up fillets; place in greased flat baking dish (12 × 8 × 2 inches). Melt 2 tablespoons butter; mix with flour. Add white wine; cook until thick. Stir in cream, salt, and brandy. Add any remaining stuffing to sauce. Pour sauce over fillets.

Bake in preheated 400°F oven about 20 to 25 minutes, until fish is done. Sprinkle with Swiss cheese the last 5 minutes of baking. The top should be golden brown. Serves 6.

mussels in white wine

3 quarts mussels
1 onion, chopped
1 shallot, chopped
2 sprigs parsley
1 sprig thyme
½ bay leaf
Pepper
¾ cup dry white wine
5 tablespoons butter
1 lemon, quartered

Scrape and scrub mussels, piling them into a large saucepan with chopped onion and shallot, parsley, thyme, bay leaf, pepper, white wine and butter.

Cover tightly; place over a high flame. After 3 minutes, stir well so mussels on top go to bottom and vice versa. Continue shaking often during cooking time of about 10 minutes. When all mussels are open, they are done.

Take mussels from pot; remove top shell of each; pile onto a hot platter; strain cooking liquid over them. Serve with lemon quarters and crisp French bread with sweet butter. Serves 3 to 4.

oysters baltimore

4 slices bacon
18 oysters
3 tablespoons chili sauce
1 tablespoon Worcestershire sauce
6 tablespoons heavy cream
½ teaspoon tarragon
2 tablespoons lemon juice
1 teaspoon salt
¼ teaspoon pepper

In medium-size skillet fry bacon until crisp. Set bacon aside to drain, then crumble into bits for garnish.

Pour off all but 1 tablespoon fat from skillet. Add oysters with their liquid. Cook uncovered over medium heat until most of pan juices are absorbed.

Mix remaining ingredients; add to oysters. Simmer no more than 5 minutes to blend all flavors. Add extra seasonings if desired.

These oysters are delicious served over hot buttered toast. Garnish with crumbled bacon. Serves 4 to 6.

oyster stuffing

1 pint oysters in own liquid (2 cups)
5 cups fresh bread crumbs
1 cup butter
1 cup chopped mild onions
½ cup sliced celery
4 tablespoons chopped parsley (½ cup)
Salt and pepper to taste
Juice of ½ lemon
A little white wine or stock

Prepare (or buy ready prepared) oysters in their own salty juice. Prepare bread crumbs made with two-day-old loaf. Melt butter; cook onions and celery until soft and light golden brown.

Add to bread crumbs, with chopped parsley and seasoning, lemon juice and oysters cut in half if large. If too dry, a little white wine or stock may be added, but stuffing must not be too soft. Fill turkey cavity; sew up carefully. Approximately 8 cups.

soft-shelled crabs

4 tablespoons butter or margarine
2 tablespoons lemon juice
6 to 8 soft-shelled crabs, cleaned
1 tablespoon cornstarch or flour
¼ cup water

Heat butter and lemon juice in medium skillet. On medium heat, cook crabs until browned, 5 minutes per side. Remove crabs to a heated platter.

Mix cornstarch and water. Add to pan juices; stir until slightly thickened. Pour sauce over crabs. Serve at once. Serves 4 to 6.

flounder with oyster sauce

1 small onion, peeled and chopped
1 carrot, peeled and chopped
1½ cups dry white wine
Salt
Peppercorns
1 bay leaf
1½ pounds flounder fillets
1½ tablespoons butter or margarine
1½ tablespoons flour
½ cup heavy cream
Paprika
1½ dozen fresh oysters
½ cup white seeded grapes

Preheat oven to 350°F. Put onion and carrot into a pan with wine; add a little salt, about 6 peppercorns and bay leaf. Simmer 15 minutes. This makes a court bouillon.

Put in fish; poach gently 7 to 10 minutes. Remove fish carefully; drain and arrange in a shallow casserole. Strain court bouillon; if there is less than 1 cup, make up the quantity with a little more wine.

Make a sauce with butter, flour and court bouillon. Add cream and paprika to taste; stir over low heat until sauce is smooth and thick. Add oysters; adjust seasoning; pour over fish.

Arrange grapes on top; cover; cook about 20 minutes. Serves 4, hot.

variation
Fresh or canned mussels can be used instead of oysters.

lobster cantonese

2 tablespoons vegetable oil
2 tablespoons black beans, rinsed, mashed
2 cloves garlic, grated
1 teaspoon grated gingerroot
2 to 3 ounces minced or ground pork
1½ to 2 pounds live lobster, cleaned and chopped into 1-inch pieces or 1 pound lobster tails, split lengthwise
1 cup chicken broth or water
1 teaspoon soy sauce
½ teaspoon sugar
1 tablespoon cornstarch in 2 tablespoons cold water
Salt and pepper
1 egg, beaten
1 scallion, sliced

Heat oil in skillet or wok; brown black beans, garlic, and ginger briefly. Add pork; stir-fry 1 minute. Add lobster; stir-fry 1 minute. Add broth, soy sauce, sugar, and cornstarch mixture. Cover; heat 5 minutes.

Remove from heat, season with salt and pepper; slowly pour in egg while stirring with a fork. This sauce should not be so hot as to completely coagulate egg and turn it white. The egg should give sauce a yellowish color.

Serve at once with rice. Garnish with scallion slices. Serves 4.

shrimp in garlic sauce

1 tablespoon vegetable oil
1 small onion, chopped
1 teaspoon freshly grated gingerroot
3 cloves garlic, minced
4 Chinese dried black mushrooms (soaked 30 minutes in warm water, drained, and sliced)
½ cup peas, fresh, or frozen and defrosted
1 pound cooked shrimps
1 cup chicken broth
2 teaspoons soy sauce
1 tablespoon cornstarch blended with 2 tablespoons water

Heat oil in frypan or wok; stir-fry onion, ginger, and garlic. Mix in mushrooms and peas; stir-fry 2 to 3 minutes. Add shrimps; continue stir-frying 1 to 2 minutes.

Combine broth, soy sauce, and cornstarch. Add to shrimp mixture; heat until sauce boils and thickens. Serve at once over boiled rice. Serves 4.

salmon soufflé

1 can salmon, red or pink
2 tablespoons butter
1 tablespoon flour
1 cup milk
1/2 teaspoon salt
Dash of freshly ground black pepper
1 teaspoon chopped chives (optional)
3 eggs, separated
2 teaspoons lemon juice

Remove dark skin and all bones from salmon. Mash with a fork.

Melt butter on top of stove; add flour; blend. Gradually add milk, stirring until sauce is slightly thickened. Add salmon to white sauce; add salt, pepper, and chives. Remove from heat.

Beat egg whites until stiff. Add beaten egg yolks and lemon juice to salmon mixture. Last, fold in stiffly beaten egg whites.

Bake mixture in a greased mold at 350°F 45 minutes. The salmon is done when a knife comes out of center clean. Serves 6.

shrimp with bean sprouts

1 green pepper (or a red, ripe one), cut into 1/4-inch strips
1 cup bean sprouts
1 teaspoon grated ginger
2 tablespoons vegetable oil
6 ounces cooked shrimps
1 tablespoon dry sherry
2 teaspoons soy sauce
Salt

Combine green pepper, bean sprouts, and ginger. Heat oil; stir-fry vegetables about 2 minutes. Push aside. Add shrimps; stir-fry until heated. Combine shrimps and vegetables; add sherry and soy sauce. Salt to taste. Serve hot with Crispy Fried Noodles. Serves 4.

crispy fried noodles
12 ounces fine egg noodles
2 cups vegetable oil for frying

Cook noodles in boiling, salted water according to package directions. Drain; rinse thoroughly in cold water. Dry on paper towels. Fry handfuls of noodles in oil at 375°F, turning frequently, about 5 minutes. Drain on paper towels. Serves 4.

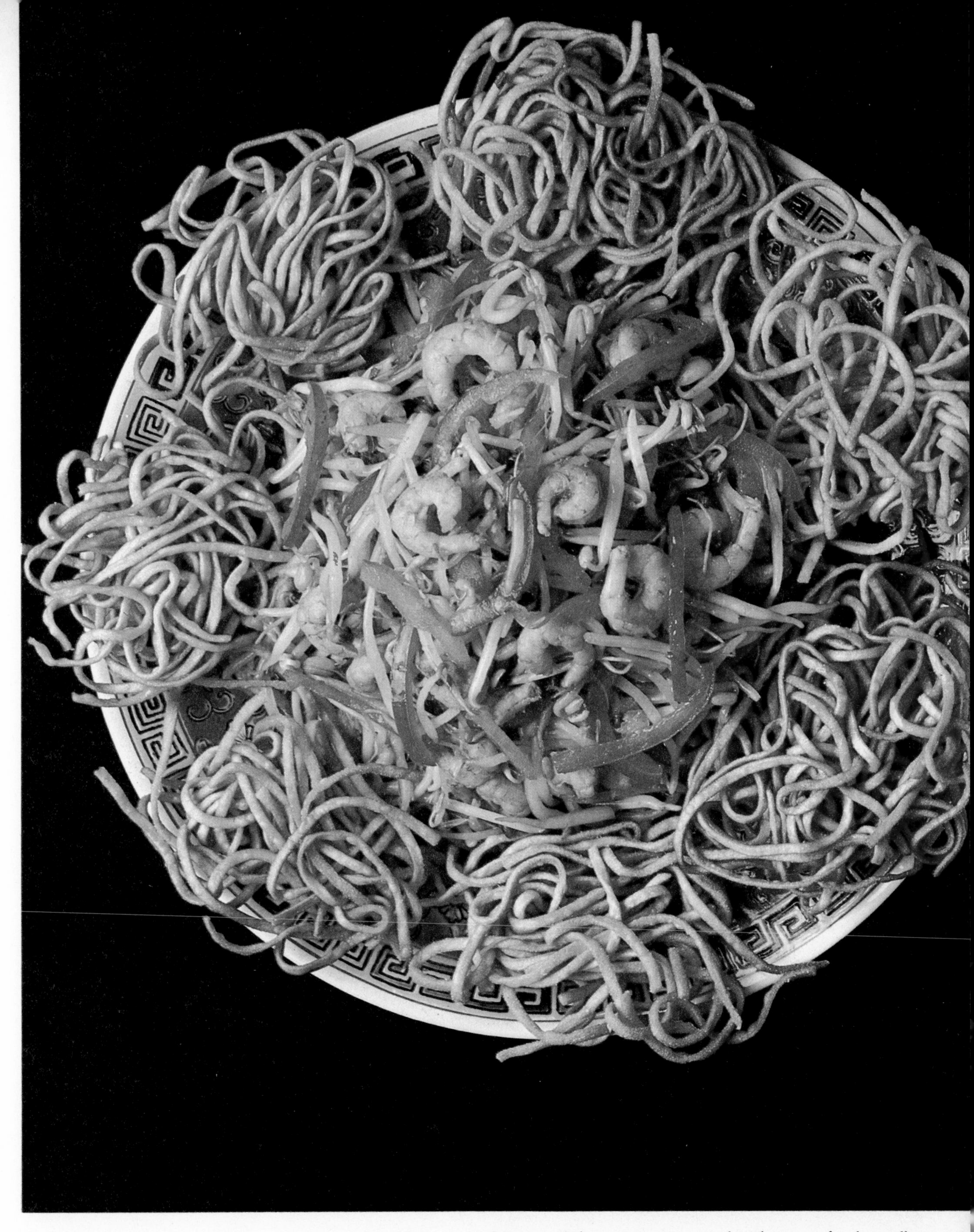

shrimp with bean sprouts served with crispy fried noodles

shrimp with marinara sauce

1 pound large shrimp (18 to 22)
1 quart water
Salt
1 bay leaf
1 slice lemon

sauce
2 tablespoons olive oil
½ cup chopped onion
1 clove garlic, minced
1½ cups Italian-style peeled plum tomatoes
¼ cup tomato puree
½ teaspoon sugar
½ teaspoon dried sweet basil, crumbled
Salt and pepper

garnish
2 tablespoons dry bread crumbs
2 tablespoons grated Parmesan cheese
1 tablespoon parsley, finely chopped

Peel and devein shrimp. Combine water, salt to taste, bay leaf and lemon in a large saucepan. Bring to a boil. Add shrimp; bring water rapidly to a boil; cook 5 minutes. Drain.

Heat oil in a heavy skillet. Add onion and garlic; sauté until tender. Break up tomatoes; add to onion and garlic along with tomato puree and seasonings. Reduce heat to low; cook uncovered 20 minutes.

Place shrimp in a lightly greased au gratin dish. Top with sauce. Combine bread crumbs, cheese and parsley; sprinkle over top of shrimp and sauce. Preheat oven to 450°F; bake 10 minutes. Serves 3.

shrimp with marinara sauce

lobster house special

3 live lobsters (about 1¾ pounds each)
⅓ cup margarine or butter
1½ cups chopped fresh mushrooms
3 tablespoons minced onion
1½ tablespoons all-purpose flour
¼ teaspoon liquid hot pepper sauce
¾ teaspoon salt
1½ cups half-and-half
3 egg yolks, beaten
3 tablespoons brandy
2 tablespoons chopped parsley
3 tablespoons fresh bread crumbs
3 tablespoons grated Parmesan cheese
½ teaspoon paprika
1 tablespoon melted margarine or butter

Place lobsters, head first, into a large pot of boiling water. Cover; simmer 15 to 20 minutes, until lobsters are done. Legs will twist off easily when done. Remove lobsters from pot. Cut off antennae. Twist off claws of lobster.

Crack and remove meat. Using scissors, cut through soft stomach shell; remove tail meat, being careful to keep shells intact. Save red coral roe, if any. Discard stomach; set aside shells. Cut lobster meat into ½-inch cubes; set aside.

In a skillet melt margarine. Add mushrooms and onion; cook until tender. Stir in flour, liquid hot pepper sauce, and salt. Gradually blend in half-and-half. Cook, stirring constantly, until thick. Add a little hot sauce to egg yolks; add to remaining sauce, stirring constantly. Heat until thickened. Stir in brandy, parsley, reserved lobster meat, and red coral roe, if any.

Divide lobster mixture into shells or ramekins. Place shells on a baking tray. Combine bread crumbs, Parmesan cheese, paprika, and margarine. Sprinkle crumb mixture over lobsters. Bake in a moderate oven, 350°F, 15 to 20 minutes or until hot. Serves 6.

lobster and rice

¼ cup butter
1 medium onion, chopped
2 cups rice
1 quart fish stock (chicken stock may be substituted)
1 bay leaf
2 tablespoons grated Parmesan cheese
2 cups cooked lobster
¼ cup sour cream
½ teaspoon salt
¼ teaspoon white pepper
¼ teaspoon paprika

Melt butter in frying pan. Add onion; cook over low heat until soft. Add rice; cook about 5 minutes, stirring constantly.

Cover with stock; bring to a boil; add bay leaf. Reduce heat; cover tightly; steam until rice is tender.

Add cheese, lobster meat, sour cream, salt, white pepper, and paprika. Serves 6.

broiled salmon steaks with herbs

4 fresh salmon steaks, 3/4 inch thick
2 tablespoons grated onion
1/3 cup butter, melted
1 teaspoon salt
1/4 teaspoon black pepper, peppermill-ground
1/2 teaspoon marjoram
1 tablespoon chopped fresh dill
2 tablespoons chopped parsley

Place salmon steaks on broiler pan.

Mix remaining ingredients; pour half of mixture over steaks. Broil 2 inches from source of heat about 4 minutes. Turn steaks. Pour remaining sauce over steaks.

Return steaks to broiler; broil an additional 6 to 7 minutes or until fish flakes. Serves 4.

sardine puff

2 cans (3 3/4 or 4 ounces each) Maine sardines
8 slices white bread
1 1/2 tablespoons butter or margarine
1/4 cup chopped green pepper
3/4 cup shredded sharp natural cheddar cheese
3 eggs
1/2 teaspoon salt
1/4 teaspoon dry mustard
Pepper to taste
2 cups milk
Paprika

Drain sardines; cut into thirds.

Remove crusts from bread; spread with butter or margarine; cut bread into 1/2-inch cubes. Place half the bread cubes in a well-greased 12 × 8 × 2-inch baking dish. Cover with sardines, green pepper, and half the cheese. Top with remaining bread cubes and cheese.

Beat eggs, salt, mustard, and pepper. Add milk; mix well. Pour over bread; sprinkle with paprika.

Bake at 350°F 45 to 50 minutes, or until firm in center. Remove from oven; let stand 5 minutes before serving. Serves 6.

dill scallops in lemon butter

1 1/2 pounds scallops
1/2 cup dry bread crumbs
8 tablespoons butter or margarine
1/4 teaspoon salt
Dash of pepper
Dash of paprika
1 tablespoon chopped parsley
2 teaspoons dillweed
3 tablespoons lemon juice

Batter scallops in bread crumbs until well-coated.

Melt 4 tablespoons butter in skillet; add salt, pepper, and paprika. Sauté scallops slowly until evenly browned, about 8 minutes. Remove scallops to a heated platter. Add remaining butter to skillet with parsley, dill, and lemon juice. Stir until hot; pour over scallops. Serve at once. Serves 4 to 6.

butterfly shrimp

1½ pounds large shrimp, cleaned and deveined, leaving tails on
¾ cup flour
1 teaspoon baking powder
½ teaspoon salt
¾ cup milk
1 egg, beaten
Fat for frying

Cut almost through shrimp lengthwise; spread out to form the butterfly. This is a trick of the knife that gets easier as you go along.

Mix flour, baking powder, and salt with milk and beaten egg. Stir until very smooth.

Heat fat in skillet. Batter each shrimp; put into hot fat. Fry until golden brown, about 7 minutes. Drain cooked shrimp on paper towels.

Serve as is or with your favorite sauce. Serves 4 to 6.

shrimp with cauliflower and chicken

1 tablespoon vegetable oil
1½ cups cauliflower, cut into florets and parboiled (cover with boiling water and let stand 5 minutes)
½ cup peas, fresh, or frozen and defrosted
½ pound cooked chicken, cubed
1 pound whole shrimps, cooked
2 scallions, cut lengthwise into thin strips

sauce
¾ cup chicken broth
1 tablespoon soy sauce
2 tablespoons chili sauce
1 tablespoon cornstarch in 2 tablespoons cold water
2 tablespoons dry white wine

Heat oil in frypan (or wok if available); stir-fry cauliflower florets 2 minutes. Remove and reserve.

Stir-fry peas 2 minutes; reserve with cauliflower.

Add chicken, shrimps, and scallions to frypan. Stir-fry 2 to 3 minutes, until heated. Return vegetables to pan.

Combine sauce ingredients; add to pan. Heat until sauce boils and thickens. Serve with rice. Serves 4.

shrimp hurry curry

1½ pounds raw, peeled, cleaned shrimp, fresh or frozen
1 can (10 ounces) frozen cream of shrimp soup
2 tablespoons butter or margarine
1 can (10½ ounces) condensed cream of mushroom soup
¾ cup sour cream
1½ teaspoons curry powder
2 tablespoons chopped parsley
Rice, toast points, or patty shells

Thaw frozen shrimp and soup. Melt butter in a 10-inch frypan. Add shrimp; cook over low heat 3 to 5 minutes, stirring frequently. Add soups; stir until thoroughly blended. Stir in cream, curry powder, and parsley. Heat. Serve over hot, fluffy rice, toast points, or in patty shells. Serves 6.

shrimp tempura

1 pound fresh large shrimp
8 ounces bamboo shoots
4 peppers, green, red, and yellow
4 small onions
2 sugared or candied ginger

tempura batter
2 ounces rice flour
6 ounces flour
1 cup water
4 jiggers rice wine or sherry
8 egg whites

4 cups oil for frying

Rinse shrimp. Drain bamboo shoots; cut into ½-inch pieces. Cut peppers into ½-inch strips. Cut onions into thick slices; separate into rings. Slice sugared ginger. Arrange these ingredients in separate small bowls.

To prepare batter, place both kinds of flour in a bowl. In a separate bowl combine water, rice wine or sherry, and egg whites until well-blended. Gradually stir into flour to form loose batter.

Heat oil in fondue pot or wok. Each person places a shrimp or piece of vegetable on a fondue fork, dips it in batter, and deep-fries it in hot oil. Serves 4.

shrimp in wine sauce

2 tablespoons butter or margarine
1 pound cooked shrimp, shelled and deveined
1 tablespoon cornstarch
1/2 teaspoon seafood seasoning
1/4 cup dry sherry
2 tablespoons water

Melt butter in medium skillet; sauté shrimp 2 minutes.

Mix cornstarch and seafood seasoning with sherry and water until very smooth. Add to shrimp; stir until sauce is thickened, about 5 minutes. Serves 4 to 6.

note
Serve this over hot rice and mop up sauce with some good French bread.

broiled scallops

1 1/2 pounds fresh or frozen scallops, defrosted
2 tablespoons honey
2 tablespoons prepared mustard
1 teaspoon curry powder
1 teaspoon lemon juice
Lemon slices

Rinse scallops; pat dry with paper towels.

Combine honey, mustard, curry, and lemon juice.

Place scallops on a broiler pan; brush with coating. Broil at 425°F, 4 inches from flame, 8 to 10 minutes or until lightly browned. Turn scallops; brush with remaining sauce. Broil 8 to 10 minutes longer. Garnish with lemon slices. Serves 6.

scallops

1 pound scallops
2 tablespoons chopped shallots or green onions
6 tablespoons butter
1 teaspoon lemon juice
1/3 cup fine bread crumbs
2 tablespoons chopped parsley

Wash scallops to remove sand; dry on paper towels. Place scallops in 4 buttered shells or in a buttered casserole.

Sauté shallots in 2 tablespoons butter until soft. Distribute evenly over scallops.

Melt remaining butter. Add lemon juice. Pour over scallops; sprinkle with crumbs. Bake in preheated 375°F oven 12 to 15 minutes, until scallops are tender when pierced with a knife. Serve scallops very hot, garnished with chopped parsley. Serves 4.

squid athenian-style

squid athenian-style

3 pounds frozen squid
1 cup chopped onions
1 clove garlic, chopped
3 tablespoons olive oil
2½ cups canned tomatoes, chopped
½ cup chopped fresh parsley
½ teaspoon salt
¼ teaspoon pepper
¾ teaspoon crumbled dried oregano
¼ cup white wine

Thaw squid. Remove tentacles; chop and reserve. Remove and discard head, chitinous pen and viscera. Wash mantle well; cut into pieces.

Sauté onion and garlic in olive oil until lightly browned. Add tomatoes, parsley, salt, pepper, oregano, wine, and squid. Cover; simmer 1 hour or until squid is tender.

Serve with rice. Serves 4 to 5.

connecticut planked shad

3- to 4-pound shad, split and boned, or other dressed fish, fresh or frozen
2 teaspoons salt
1/8 teaspoon pepper
1/4 cup melted margarine or butter

Thaw fish if frozen. Sprinkle inside and outside with salt and pepper. Place fish, skin-side-down, on a well-greased plank or baking tray. Brush with melted margarine. Bake in a 350°F oven 40 to 60 minutes or until fish flakes.

Spread soufflé over fish. Return to oven; bake 10 to 15 minutes longer or until soufflé is done and browned. Serves 6.

soufflé

1/4 cup margarine or butter
1/4 cup minced onion
1/2 cup all-purpose flour
1/2 teaspoon salt
1 cup milk
1/4 cup white wine
1 tablespoon lemon juice
3 egg yolks, beaten
1/2 cup chopped parsley
3 egg whites, beaten until stiff
1 jar (3 1/2 ounces) caviar, optional

In a saucepan, melt margarine. Add onion; cook until tender. Blend in flour and salt. Gradually stir in milk, wine, and lemon juice. Cook until thickened, stirring constantly. Blend a little hot sauce into egg yolks; add to remaining sauce, stirring constantly. Heat just until mixture thickens. Stir in chopped parsley. Fold in egg whites and caviar.

note
If fresh shad roe is available, cook in salted vinegar water. Remove membrane; use in place of caviar.

maryland shad

1 4-pound shad, dressed
Salt and freshly ground pepper to taste
Lemon and pepper seasoning
3 cups water
1 cup white wine
2 ribs celery, broken into pieces
1 tablespoon instant minced onion or 1 small onion, chopped
2 bay leaves

Preheat oven to 300°F.

Wash shad; dry with paper towels. Sprinkle fish inside and out with salt, pepper, and lemon and pepper seasoning.

Put fish on rack of a baking pan. Add water and wine to level just under fish. Add remaining ingredients.

Cover tightly; steam 5 hours. Baste often. Serves 6.

note
This shad is over-steamed, so you even eat the bones.

scallops with mushrooms

1½ pounds scallops
½ cup butter
1 cup dry white wine
½ teaspoon salt
⅛ teaspoon pepper
1 green onion, minced
4 tablespoons flour
1 cup heavy cream
1 cup milk
½ pound fresh mushrooms, sliced
Drops of lemon juice
Salt and pepper to taste
1 tablespoon cognac
2 tablespons butter
6 scallop shells or pyrex dishes
Roe for garnish (optional)

Wash scallops well in slightly salted water to remove all grit. Drain; dry on paper towels. Cut scallops in half or in fourths to make them bite-size.

In medium saucepan bring ½ cup butter, wine, ½ teaspoon salt, ⅛ teaspoon pepper, and onion to simmer. Add scallops; return to simmer. Cover; simmer slowly 5 minutes. Remove scallops with slotted spoon; set aside.

Boil pan liquids; reduce to just butter. Add flour; cook, stirring, 3 minutes. Stir in cream, milk, mushrooms, lemon juice, and salt and pepper to taste. Over medium heat, cook until thickened, stirring frequently. Add cognac. Blend two-thirds of sauce with scallops.

Grease shells or dishes. Divide scallop mixture between them. Cover with rest of sauce. Dot with 2 tablespoons butter. Just before serving, place in preheated 400°F oven; heat about 10 minutes or until sauce is bubbling. Garnish with roe, if available. Serves 6.

scallop kabobs

1 pound scallops, fresh or frozen
1 can (13½ ounces) pineapple chunks, drained
1 can (4 ounces) button mushrooms, drained
1 green pepper, cut into 1-inch squares
¼ cup melted fat or oil
¼ cup lemon juice
¼ cup chopped parsley
¼ cup soy sauce
½ teaspoon salt
Dash of pepper
12 slices bacon

Thaw frozen scallops. Rinse with cold water to remove any shell particles.

Place pineapple, mushrooms, green pepper, and scallops in a bowl. Combine fat, lemon juice, parsley, soy sauce, salt, and pepper. Pour sauce over scallop mixture; let stand 30 minutes, stirring occasionally.

Fry bacon until cooked but not crisp. Cut each slice in half. Using long skewers, alternate scallops, pineapple, mushrooms, green pepper, and bacon until skewers are filled.

Cook about 4 inches from moderately hot coals 5 minutes. Baste with sauce. Turn and cook 5 to 7 minutes longer or until bacon is crisp. Serves 6.

Index

T

V

W